Meet the Shapes

Diamond loves a windy day.

Circle finds a place to play.

Oval bakes a
tasty treat.

Octagon lands
on both feet.

Square builds it
up so high.

Star flies through the sky.

Triangle likes to share with friends.

Rectangle shines
as each day ends.

Take a look around
your street,

you never know what
shapes you'll meet.

The End

Preschool Prep Company®

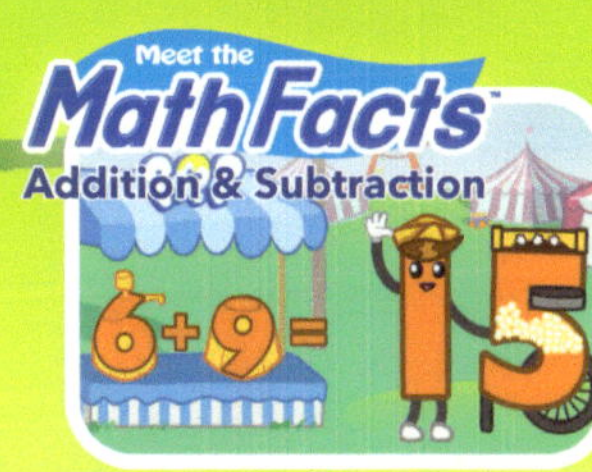

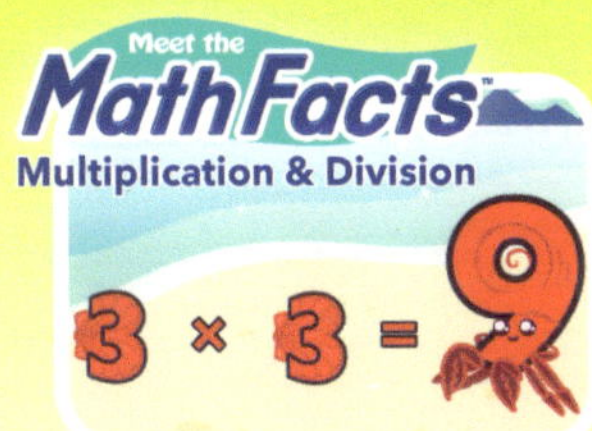

Videos • Workbooks • Flashcards • Easy Reader Books • Coloring Books
Kits • Board Books • Lift the Flap Books • Apps • eBooks • Downloads

Download Our Award-Winning Videos!

www.preschoolprep.com

www.preschoolpreponline.com (International)

www.ingramcontent.com/pod-product-compliance
Ingram Content Group UK Ltd.
Pitfield, Milton Keynes, MK11 3LW, UK
UKHW060403300726
14090UKWH00001B/108
9798887210322